Controlling An Inverted Pendulum Using Microcontroller

Martine Maradona

Controlling An Inverted Pendulum Using Microcontroller

LAP LAMBERT Academic Publishing

Impressum / Imprint
Bibliografische Information der Deutschen Nationalbibliothek: Die Deutsche Nationalbibliothek verzeichnet diese Publikation in der Deutschen Nationalbibliografie; detaillierte bibliografische Daten sind im Internet über http://dnb.d-nb.de abrufbar.
Alle in diesem Buch genannten Marken und Produktnamen unterliegen warenzeichen-, marken- oder patentrechtlichem Schutz bzw. sind Warenzeichen oder eingetragene Warenzeichen der jeweiligen Inhaber. Die Wiedergabe von Marken, Produktnamen, Gebrauchsnamen, Handelsnamen, Warenbezeichnungen u.s.w. in diesem Werk berechtigt auch ohne besondere Kennzeichnung nicht zu der Annahme, dass solche Namen im Sinne der Warenzeichen- und Markenschutzgesetzgebung als frei zu betrachten wären und daher von jedermann benutzt werden dürften.

Bibliographic information published by the Deutsche Nationalbibliothek: The Deutsche Nationalbibliothek lists this publication in the Deutsche Nationalbibliografie; detailed bibliographic data are available in the Internet at http://dnb.d-nb.de.
Any brand names and product names mentioned in this book are subject to trademark, brand or patent protection and are trademarks or registered trademarks of their respective holders. The use of brand names, product names, common names, trade names, product descriptions etc. even without a particular marking in this work is in no way to be construed to mean that such names may be regarded as unrestricted in respect of trademark and brand protection legislation and could thus be used by anyone.

Coverbild / Cover image: www.ingimage.com

Verlag / Publisher:
LAP LAMBERT Academic Publishing
ist ein Imprint der / is a trademark of
OmniScriptum GmbH & Co. KG
Heinrich-Böcking-Str. 6-8, 66121 Saarbrücken, Deutschland / Germany
Email: info@lap-publishing.com

Herstellung: siehe letzte Seite /
Printed at: see last page
ISBN: 978-3-659-67000-8

ABSTRACT

Controlling an Inverted Pendulum Using Microcontroller

By

Martine Maradona

SWISS GERMAN UNIVERSITY

Bumi Serpong Damai

Dr. –Ing. Ir. Yul Y. Nazaruddin MSc., Major Advisor

Inverted pendulum is an example of naturally unstable system. In order to stabilize an inverted pendulum, a proper controller should be used. One of the famous controllers is PID [1]). PID controller can be analog (consist of several operational amplifiers) or digital.

In this thesis, a microcontroller is used as a digital PID controller. The real PID formula contains a differentials equation. An 8-bit microcontroller is not fast enough to calculate such formula within a short time (less than 10ms). Therefore, the formula should be first simplified; hence, the microcontroller can perform the computation in a tight timing.

The actuator for this inverted pendulum is a DC motor. The speed of the motor is controlled using PWM (Pulse Width Modulator).

The main purpose of this thesis is to develop a PID controller using a microcontroller. The second purpose is to provide students an experimental tool in order to understand what PID controller is. In addition, the third purpose of this thesis is to provide SGU laboratory with an inverted pendulum.

---

[1])PID is a standard feedback loop component in industrial control applications.

Martine Maradona

DEDICATION

This thesis is dedicated to my parents and my sister.

---

[1])PID is a standard feedback loop component in industrial control applications.

Martine Maradona

ACKNOWLEDGEMENTS

The author wishes to thank Dr. Yul Y. Nazaruddin MSc. for his guidance during the thesis work, Dipl. –Ing Maralo Sinaga, Ir. Arko, PhD, Edward B. Manurung M. Eng and my parents for his general advice and finally, all lecturers and staffs in Swiss German University who have given their knowledge and support to build this final project work.

The author also wishes to thank all colleagues in Swiss German University and everyone who has supported the thesis work.

Without all those listed above, this thesis would not have been completed.

TABLE OF CONTENTS

LIST OF TABLES

LIST OF EQUATIONS

LIST OF FIGURES

Chapter 1 – Introduction

1.1. Background

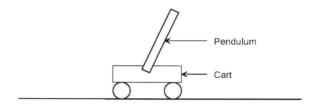

Figure 1.1. Sketch of an inverted pendulum

A normal single axis inverted pendulum consists of two main parts. They are a cart and a pendulum, which is inversely placed. The cart is connected to the DC motor, thus the cart can move to the left or right. The pendulum can fall freely to the left or right. The goal is to maintain the pendulum in vertical position, by moving the cart to the left or to the right.

Inverted pendulum has been used for a long time as a measuring tool of a controller's performance.

1.2. Research problem

The main problem in this thesis is to implement PID controller in an inverted pendulum using a microcontroller. Usually PID controller is composed of several operational amplifiers, resistors, and capacitors. However, in this thesis a program is used as a replacement of operational amplifier. In other words, the PID controller is implemented in digital design.

1.3. Research purpose

The first purpose of this thesis is implementing digital PID controller in a microcontroller. The second purpose is to provide students an experimental tool in order to understand what PID controller is. In addition, the third purpose of this thesis is to provide SGU laboratory with an inverted pendulum.

1.4. Thesis scope

The scope of this thesis is including hardware design, software design, and electronic design.

1.5. Thesis structure

This thesis was written according to the following structure:

Chapter 1 – Introduction

Chapter 2 – Literature review

Chapter 3 – Methodology

Chapter 4 – Result and discussion

Chapter 5 – Conclusion and recommendation

Chapter 2 – Literature review

2.1. PID controller

The main purpose of a controller is to maintain the output, so the output has no difference with desired output value. PID controller can be used to control flow rate, speed and other variables.

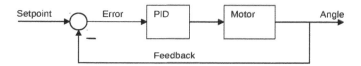

Figure 2.1. Inverted pendulum closed loop system

As shown in figure 2.1., PID is used as a controller. This PID controller will then be implemented in the microcontroller. The equation for PID can be written as

$$c(t) = Kpe(t) + Ki\int_0^t e(t)dt + Kde(t)\frac{d}{d(t)}$$

Equation 2.1. PID equation in time domain [2]

As shown at above equation, PID controller contains three parts, proportional part, integral part, and derivative part. Every part is summed together to get an output of the PID controller. The controller reaction is based on error e(t), proportional constant (Kp), integral constant (Ki), and derivative constant (Kd). The error itself is

Error = setpoint – measured value

"Setpoint" is the desired value and "measured value" is feedback value from sensor.

Applying PID equation directly to the microcontroller is very difficult, because it is an equation with integral and derivative. A modification should be done before the equation can be calculated in the microcontroller.

A modification to the PID equation results the following equation

$$c(n) = Kp * e(n) + Ki * \sum_{i=0}^{n} e(n) * \Delta t + Kd \frac{e(n) - e(n-1)}{\Delta t}$$

Equation 2.2. PID equation in digital [7]

The above equation is the digital version of the continues time of the above first PID controller equation and therefore this equation is implemented in the microcontroller.

2.2. Microcontroller

Microcontroller is microprocessor with internal ROM (Read Only Memory), RAM (Random Access Memory), timer, and sometimes ADC (Analog to Digital Converter). Because of their features, microcontrollers are used in many systems that require uncomplicated logic operations and simple calculations. Actually, microprocessor can also be used, but RAM, ROM, and PPI (Programmable Peripheral Interface) should be added. Those external devices are not practical and cost more money.

In the market, there are many types of microcontrollers. Each type of microcontroller has its own set of code to command the microcontroller. That set of code is called instruction set.

One of the most famous microcontrollers is MCS-51™. Intel® manufactured MCS-51™ in 1980. Now, after two decades, some manufacturers such as Atmel® produce microcontrollers that have the same core. That kind of microcontrollers is called 8051 family.

Besides Atmel®, there are many more microcontrollers' manufacturer, such as Freescale Semiconductor®, Parallax®, Microchip®, ZiLOG®, Cypress MicroSystems® and Texas Instruments®. They create their own microcontrollers. Their microcontrollers have unique instruction set and architecture.

Microcontrollers produced by different manufacturer offer different features and advantages. It depends on the requirement of the system, which microcontroller should be chosen.

Atmel® AVR™

In addition to 8051 family, Atmel® also produces several microcontroller families. One of the families is AVR™. AVR™ is an 8-bit RISC (Reduced Instruction Set Computing) microcontroller with Harvard architecture. RISC microcontrollers take advantages of smaller and simpler instruction set. And Harvard architecture means separate pathway for instruction and data. This architecture supports the microcontroller to do a single cycle operations.

The AVR™ family has several subfamilies, which are tinyAVR™, megaAVR™, USB AVR™, and LCD AVR™. The family used in this thesis is megaAVR™.

The acronym AVR has been reported/rumored to stand for Advanced Virtual RISC and/or the initials of the two company founders—Alf Egil Bogen and Vegard Wollan—who for their part have chosen to let the matter rest unresolved, giving mostly shadowy answers when asked directly. [19]

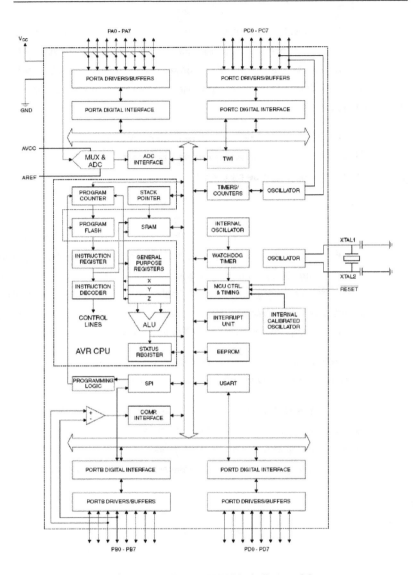

Figure 2.2. ATmega 8535 block diagram [4]

Development Board

A development board is a PCB that contains microcontroller, power supply, reset circuit, RS-232 line driver, and many other thing that support the microcontroller to become ready to be used for developing a project.

Development board that is used in this thesis is DT-AVR Low Cost Micro System™. This board is designed and assembled by Innovative Electronics®. ATmega 8535, as a part of megaAVR™ family, is used as the core part.

This development board is chosen because this board matches the requirement for developing digital controller. See chapter 3.1. for more detail reasons.

2.3. LCD (Liquid Crystal Display) and driver

If a simple visualization is needed, LCD is the right choice.

There are two types of dot matrix LCD, character and graphic. Character LCD can only display characters. Usually the size of this LCD is counted by how many character can be displayed.

A graphic LCD can display characters and pictures. The size of a graphic LCD is counted by how many pixels can be displayed.

LCD used in this thesis is GM24644. This LCD is a graphic LCD produced by Data Image. GM24644 is powered with T6963C from Toshiba® as LCD controller. This chip communicates with the microprocessor/microcontroller using parallel communication. This type of communication is easier to program, but I/O consuming.

Table 2.1. GM24644 pin description [8]

Pin
is

Pin	Symbol	Function
1	Vss	Ground
2	FGND	Frame ground
3	NC	Not connected
4	Vdd	Supply voltage (+5v)
5	$\overline{RD}$	Data read
6	$\overline{RW}$	Data write
7	$C/\overline{D}$	Command/data
8	$\overline{CE}$	Chip enable
9	$\overline{RESET}$	Chip reset
10	PWM	Pulse width modulation for LCD contrast
11	DB1	
12	DB0	
13	DB3	
14	DB2	Data bus line
15	DB5	
16	DB4	
17	DB7	
18	DB6	
19	NC	Not connected
20	FS	Font select, L=8x8, H=8x6

10

replaced with variable resistor. This action will reduce the needs of pin from microcontroller. Large font is used, therefore pin 20 is connected to ground.

This pin configuration will reduce the pin required by LCD to 13, which are five for control and eight for data, as shown in figure 2.3.

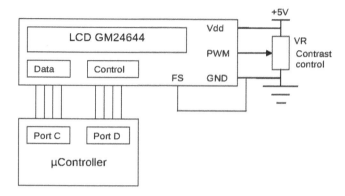

Figure 2.3. LCD GM24644 connection

2.4. DC motor

There are many types of DC motors. In this thesis, a "permanent magnet" brushed type is used.

The stator fields in permanent magnet motors are provided by permanent magnets. In order to reverse the direction of a "permanent magnet motor" direction, the voltage polarity should be reversed.

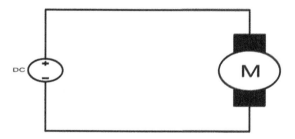

Figure 2.4. DC motor schematic diagram

2.5. PWM (Pulse Width Modulation)

If digital controller is used, the easiest way to control the motor's speed and direction is by using a PWM (Pulse Width Modulation) technique.

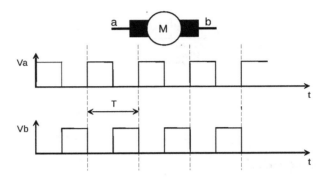

Figure 2.5. PWM pulse [1]

Figure 2.5. shows that voltage that come in to point a and point b is always complemented. By maintaining the duty cycle at 50%, the motor will not move.

Care should be taken when selecting the PWM frequency. For typical motor application the frequency should not less than 60 Hz, or higher than 1000 Hz. Lower than 60 Hz could cause big vibration, and higher than 1000 Hz could lead to high switching loss. [1]

To change direction or speed of the motor, the duty cycle should be changed. Figure 2.6. shows how the direction of the motor can be altered.

At figure 2.6.a duty cycle at point a = 25 %, the duty cycle at point b should be 75%. At this condition, the motor will turn forward. If the duty cycle at point a is reduced to 10% (automatically duty cycle at point b become 90%) the motor will turn forward faster. If the duty cycle at point a is increased to 45%, the motor will run forward with slow speed.

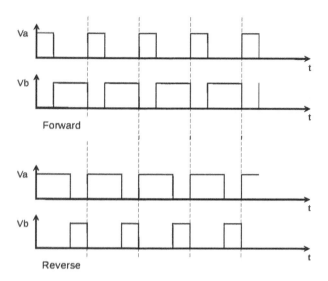

Figure 2.6. PWM forward and reverse [1]

DC motor is chosen because it is easy to be controlled. Only one wire is needed for controlling speed and direction of the motor.

2.6. DC motor driver (H-Bridge)

It is impossible to drive a motor directly from microcontroller. Because the current can be pulled from microcontroller is relatively small. Output from microcontroller should only be used for information, and not for power. A device is needed to interface between DC motor and microcontroller. The device is called motor driver.

A simple driver for DC motor can be made using H-Bridge circuit.

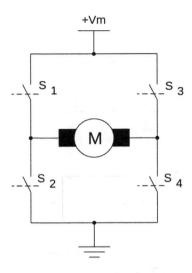

Figure 2.7. H-Bridge

S1 and S4 are a switch pair, and so with S2 and S3. They are called pairs because they always conduct at the same time. S1 and S2 never conduct at the same time, and so with S3 and S4. If they are conduct at the same time, it is called short circuit.

When S1 and S4 conduct, the motor will turn to a specific direction. Then, if S2 and S3 conduct, the direction of the motor will be reversed.

H-Bridge can work with PWM. To be able to work with PWM, S1 and S4 must be connected to PWM channel, and S2 and S3 must be connected to inverse PWM channel. (See chapter 2.5. for more detail about PWM).

Many semiconductor manufacturers built a single IC for driving motor. The driver usually receives information from microcontroller in logic level, and converts them into a high power output.

Some examples of motor driver in IC are LMD18200 from National Semiconductor®, L293B/D/E from STMicroelectronics®, and L298N from STMicroelectronics®.

The motor driver used in this thesis is L298N. The total current can be drawn from L298N is 4 A.

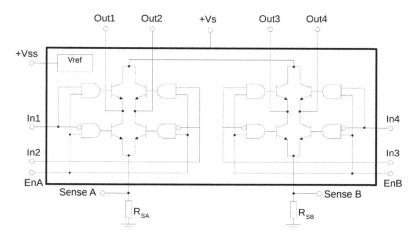

Figure 2.8. L298N block diagram [10]

As shown is figure 2.8. the lower transistors are connected together and correspond to external resistors (R_{SA} and R_{SB}). Therefore, the presence of external resistors connected to the ground is important.

2.7. Potentiometer as a sensor

Potentiometer is a variable resistor with three terminals that the resistance can be adjusted. The resistance of middle terminal of the potentiometer can be adjusted with reference of other terminal.

A potentiometer can be used as a displacement sensor by connecting the middle terminal to signal processor, and the other two to supply voltage.

The typical application of potentiometer as a movement sensor is as follow

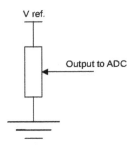

Figure 2.9. Potentiometer as a displacement sensor

2.8. Serial communication

Serial communication is a method of sending information one bit at a time. Because of that, serial communication requires less cable than parallel communication. However, as the compensation, serial communication is slower than parallel communication (if both communications have the same frequency).

One of the most famous serial communications is RS-232. RS-232 is a type of asynchronous serial communication, which means the clock is generated in each device (transmitter and receiver), instead of generated only by one device, and sent the clock through the clock bus.

In this thesis, RS-232 is used to send data from microcontroller to a computer.

2.9. ISP (In System Programmable) Microcontroller programming

Before get started with the real programming, the fuse bit in the new ATmega 8535 microcontroller should be first programmed. This action can be done using CodeVisionAVR™ from HP Info Tech®.

CodeVisionAVR™ is an IDE (Integrated Development Environment) for the Atmel® AVR™ family of microcontrollers. Although CodeVisionAVR™ has complete functions for program developing, program debugging, and chip programmer, but in this thesis, CodeVisionAVR™ will only be used as a chip programmer. Compiler and debugger in CodeVisionAVR™ are not used, because this compiler can only handle C source.

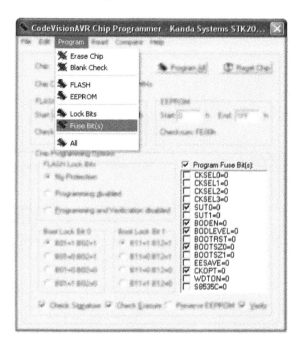

Figure 2.10. Chip programmer

Figure 2.10. shows CodeVisionAVR™ Chip Programmer. It has the ability to read and write flash memory, EEPROM (Electrically Erasable Programmable Read Only Memory), lock bits and fuse bits.

The fuse bits setting that are used for this thesis is as shown in figure 2.4. Fuse bit that has a check sign means programmed (0), and fuse bit that has no check sign means unprogrammed (1).

After the fuse bits are programmed, the microcontroller is ready to be used. The next step is building a program. In this thesis, AVR Studio 4™ is used for compiling, debugging, and simulating.

Figure 2.11. AVR Studio 4™

Figure 2.11. is the view of AVR studio. AVR studio 4™ has three main windows.

Window number one is called workspace window. This window contains files that are related to the project, I/O (that is used for debugging), and information of microcontroller that is currently simulated.

Window number two is source editor window. The source code in assembly language is edited here.

Window number three is output window. This window is functioned as messages, which come out from compiler. For example, if a command is mistyped in source editor window, AVR Studio 4™ will display the error in this window.

Chapter 3 – Methodology

3.1. Processing unit selection

There are several options for the processing unit. The requirements for the processing unit are:

Processing speed

The sampling time for the system is 66.6 milliseconds. In other word, in one second there will be 15 samples. Between each sample, acquiring error from the sensor and calculating PID should be done. The processing unit must be fast enough to do it.

Internal ADC

An internal ADC would be preferred, because it will decrease the needs of external device. Moreover, the communication between the ADC and processing unit will be simpler.

Hardware UART (Universal Asynchronous Receiver Transmitter)

Emulating RS-232 in software will waste more time, therefore processing unit with hardware USART will help much.

Development board

If available, it is better to pick processing unit + development board. With processing unit + development board, the time to design and assemble development board can be eliminated. That will give extra time for other activity.

Processing units that match the requirements are microcontroller or DSP. Since DSP chip is more expensive and cannot be found easily, the microcontroller is the wise choice. In the market, the types of microcontroller that come with development board are limited. They are DT-51™, DT-AVR™, and DT-Basic™. All of them are produced by Innovative Electronics®.

DT-51™ uses at89s51 as the microcontroller; DT-AVR™ uses ATmega 8535 as the microcontroller; and DT-Basic™ uses Basic Stamp™ as the microcontroller. The development board that matches very close to the requirements is DT-AVR™. ATmega 8535 has internal ADC, hardware multiplier, and hardware USART (Universal Synchronous Asynchronous Receiver Transmitter). Moreover, AVR™ core microcontroller needs only one clock to do one operation (single cycle operation). This feature makes AVR™ faster than 8051 family that requires 12 clocks to do one operation.

3.2. Angle sensor selection

There are two options for angle sensor, using encoder or using potentiometer. Potentiometer was chosen because of its cost.

A linear type of rotary potentiometer is preferred, since the input is angle.

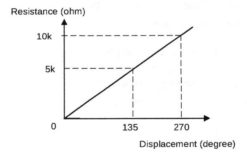

Figure 3.1. Linear potentiometer

3.3. First version of the inverted pendulum

3.3.1. Mechanical design

The first design of the inverted pendulum is linear.

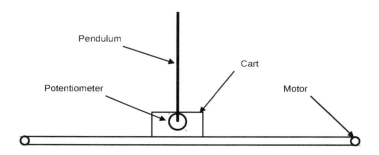

Figure 3.2. First version of inverted pendulum mechanical design

The mechanic body of this inverted pendulum is made up from 90% dot matrix printer. Since the printer was A3 size, the pendulum should have enough space to move. A stepper motor from the printer is used to drive the cart.

3.3.2. Electrical design

For the power supply, a regulator IC is used. Since the current consumption for the stepper motor is low (500mA at 12 volt), a typical application of 78xx regulator is enough.

3.3.3. Software design

A simple program is developed to control the chart. The program contains only a few logic operations.

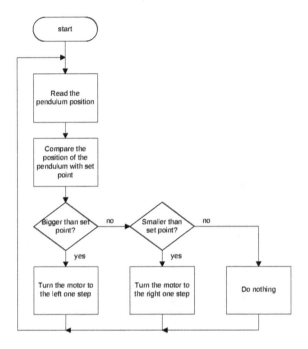

Figure 3.3. First version of inverted pendulum software design

3.4. Second version of the inverted pendulum

3.4.1. Mechanical design

There is no significant change in mechanical design from the first version. A minor change is happened to the actuator. This second version uses DC motor as the actuator.

3.4.2. Electrical design

Since the current requirement is increase up to 1200mA, the power supply from the first version should be modified. A transistor as current amplifier is added.

Besides power supply, the motor driver also needs some modification. The old H-bridge IC (L293D) supports until 600mA.

In DC motor driver circuit, an inverter is used because PWM require two inputs that always complemented (See chapter 2.5. for more detail about why complemented input is needed). PWM signal produced by microcontroller is branched in to two. The first goes through inverter then to the IC driver, and the second one goes directly to the IC driver. The inverter used in this thesis is 74LS04. Only one channel of six channels of this inverter is used. Four schottky diodes are used because the L298N driving inductive loads at high frequency.

3.4.3. Software design

The software needs to be redesign completely. At this version, PID controller will be implemented in software.

Here is the pseudo code to calculate PID

```
Error = Setpoint - measured value
Proportional = Kp * Error
SumError = SumError + Error
Integral = Ki * SumError * t
Derivative = Kd * (Error - LastError) / t
LastError = Error
PID = Proportional + Integral + Derivative
```

Kp, Ki and Kd are constants; t is sampling time. (See chapter 2.1. for more information about implementing PID in digital).

All variables are in 8-bit sign integer. The use of 8-bit sign integer makes the programming in assembly not complicated.

If the program is run smoothly, the variables can be changed to 16-bit sign integer or even floating point to avoid overflow.

Timer 2 in microcontroller controls when interrupt subroutine should occur. If Interrupt occurs, microcontroller reads the error, and then calculates PID based on the error, after PWM duty cycle is updated. The process is always repeated. The time needed from reading the first error to reading the second error is called sampling time. The sampling frequency should be high enough so that the aliasing effect will not happen.

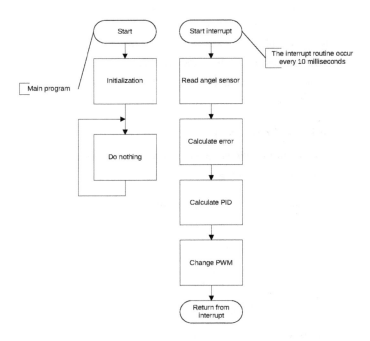

Figure 3.4. Second version of inverted pendulum software

3.5. Third version of the inverted pendulum

3.5.1. Mechanical design

The system consists of three main parts, the base (board), the cart, and the pendulum itself. The cart is made from zinc. It has two wheels, one of which is attached to the DC motor. In the cart, there are a potentiometer and 8mm female stereo jack (to connect between base and cart).

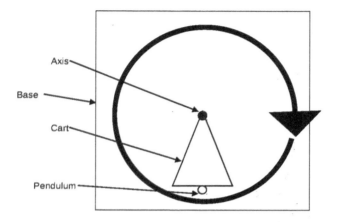

Figure 3.5. Top view of circular inverted pendulum

A circular inverted pendulum gives another problem to the connections. Since, there are turning part (the cart and the pendulum), the connection between microcontroller and pendulum (sensor), also motor driver and DC motor cannot be connected directly using cable. Special connectors should be used to join between rotating part and static part. The normal connection without connectors will make the cables twisted.

There are two possibilities of solution for this problem. The first one is to move all the devices above the cart. This solution will leave only 3 connections, which are 9 volt (for microcontroller), 15 volt (for DC motor), and ground. These three connections can be easily overcome using 8mm stereo jack. Since there will be LCD, it would be not wise to put LCD in the moving object.

The second choice is to leave only potentiometer and motor in the cart. This solution increase the total connections needed to five, which are, three for potentiometer and two for DC motor. The three cables for potentiometer can be handled by 8mm stereo jack.

3.5.2. Electrical design

There are no changes in electrical design. The design from the second version is reused here.

3.5.3. Software design

The main core of the program is still the same as the second version. Some minor changes are made to increase the performance.

16-bit sign integer is used, as an improvement from the previous version. Moreover, the PID constants (Kp, Ki, and Kd) can be adjusted real time. This improvement makes the changing of PID constants more comfortable.

LCD and serial communication are added to make the monitoring process become easier.

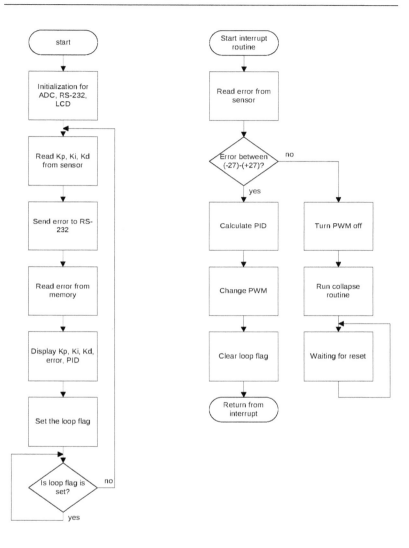

Figure 3.6. Third version of inverted pendulum software

3.5.3.1. Displaying the result to the LCD

The LCD (T6963C) is used as the display of Proportional constant, integral constant, derivative constant, error, and controller response.

In microcontroller, all variable (Kp, Ki, Kd, error, etc) are saved in 16-bit, or one word. This variable cannot be sent directly to the LCD, because all variable in microcontroller are interpreted as sign integer. Unfortunately, LCD interprets all the incoming data as character code. The character code that used in T6963C is not the same as ASCII (American Standard Code for International Interchange). Therefore, the data should be first converted into ASCII and than shift the code until match the character code in T6963C

Below, at figure 3.7. is the flowchart how 8-bit unsign integer is converted into ASCII.

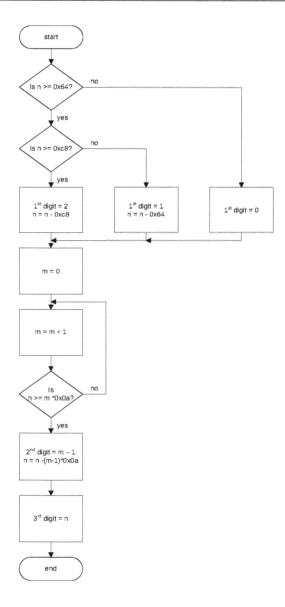

Figure 3.7. Integer to ASCII flowchart

3.5.3.2. RS-232 communication

Since ATmega 8535 has hardware USART, the serial communication became very easy. The thing that must be done is configuring the USART, and then just put the data that want to be sent to a given register.

Here is the complete assembly code to initialize USART

```
ldi templ, 12
out ubrrl, templ
ldi templ, 0
out ubrrh, templ
ldi templ, (1<<ursel)|(2<<upm0)|
(1<<usbs)|(3<<ucsz0)
out ucsrc, templ
ldi templ, (1<<txen)
out ucsrb, templ
```

The meaning of each line is explained below:

```
ldi templ, 12
out ubrrl, templ
ldi templ, 0
out ubrrh, templ
```

These four lines set the baud rate that will be used in serial communication. The baud rate can be calculated using the formula below

$$Baudrate = \frac{fosc}{16(ubrr+1)} \qquad \text{or}$$

$$ubrr = \frac{fosc}{16*baudrate} - 1$$

Equation 3.1. Formula for baudrate [4]

fosc=system clock frequency

baudrate=baud rate in bps (bit per second)

ubrr=value for ubrrh and ubrrl registers

System clock frequency that currently used is 4 MHz, and the desired baud rate is 19200.

$$ubrr = \frac{4x10^6}{16x19200} - 1$$
$$ubrr = \frac{4x10^6}{307200} - 1$$
$$ubrr = 12,0208 \approx 12$$

From the equation, the value for ubrrh and ubrrl is 12. Since 12 are lower than 255, only ubrrl is filled, and ubrrh is zero.

```
out ubrrh, temp1
ldi temp1, (1<<ursel)|(2<<upm0)|
(1<<usbs)|(3<<ucsz0)
```

This line define the communication as asynchronous, even parity, 2 stop bits, 8-character size. Because RS-232 is asynchronous communication, the setting in microcontroller should also asynchronous.

```
ldi temp1, (1<<txen)
out ucsrb, temp1
```

This line enables the transmitter. The pin that usually used as general I/O is now overridden as USART transmitter.

After the initialization is complete, to send an 8-bit data, just put the data at register UDR. For example:

```
out udr, r18
```

This command tells the microcontroller to send the value in r18 through USART.

Chapter 4 – Result and discussion

4.1. Result of the first version

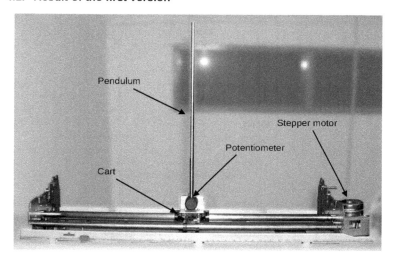

Figure 4.1. Mechanical result of the first version

The mechanical part works perfectly, because it is a printer mechanic.

Problem does not occur during power supply test. The voltage is stable at 12 volt.

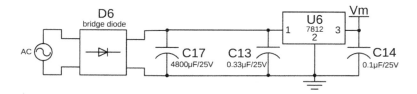

Figure 4.2. Twelve-volt power supply [9]

To test the stepper motor driver the following signal is given in sequence:

1010, 0010, 0110, 0100, 0101, 0001, 1001, 1000.

The stepper motor turns faster if the delay between each signal is decreased.

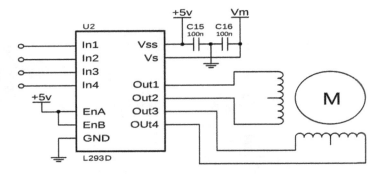

Figure 4.3. Stepper motor driver

Each part of the inverted pendulum (sensor and stepper motor) works perfectly. The sensor's output can be read by the microcontroller, and the motor can be controlled.

Unfortunately, the first version of the inverted pendulum is not stable at all, not even a second. The pendulum falls after one or two oscillations. From this trial, It is clear that the real controller was needed, not only a simple logic operation.

4.2. Result of the second version

Mechanical part is not changed, but electrical part; especially for power supply and motor driver is changed.

The output voltage is varying between 17.8 volt at no load and 18.4 volt when the DC motor is connected. The voltage difference is acceptable, since the motor is not sensitive to the small voltage change.

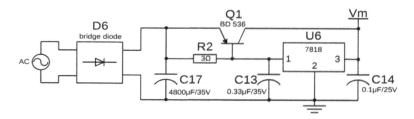

Figure 4.4. High current power supply [9]

For the DC motor driver, the main component is H-Bridge IC L298N from STMicroelectronics®. A heat sink is used to cool down this IC.

A test for DC motor driver is done by connecting the PWM port to square wave generator with 50% duty cycle. No anomalies occur during test, the DC motor does not turn, only vibrating.

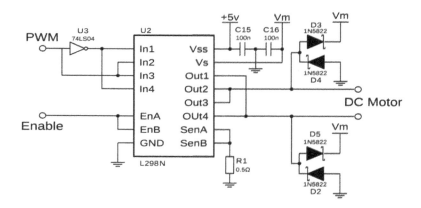

Figure 4.5. DC motor driver

The big modification gives an improvement to the pendulum stability. The pendulum can stand, but actively shift to the left or to the right. After some seconds the pendulum reached the end, and fall. This active movement occurs because of the vibration of the duet DC motor and PWM. The vibrations move through the cart and disturb the settled pendulum, so the pendulum away from its setpoint. The cart tries to balance the pendulum, but again the vibrations make pendulum out from its setpoint. This situation happens continuously and causes the chart to shift actively.

To deal with this problem, the idea is to make a circular or a rotary inverted pendulum.

4.3. Result of the third version

The stability of inverted pendulum has no difference with the second version. Small oscillations always occur because of DC motor vibration.

As already mentioned in chapter 3.5.1., the 8mm stereo jack makes the connection from microcontroller and potentiometer not perfect. The friction while the cart is turning could generate unstable supply voltage for the potentiometer. Stable supply for potentiometer is significant, because a slight difference could make an error to PID calculation. To improve voltage stability, a capacitor is used.

Figure 4.6. Potentiometer with capacitor

The connection between rotating part and static part is solved. Five connections (two for motor and three for potentiometer) are tested and work. The detail five connections can be seen at figure below.

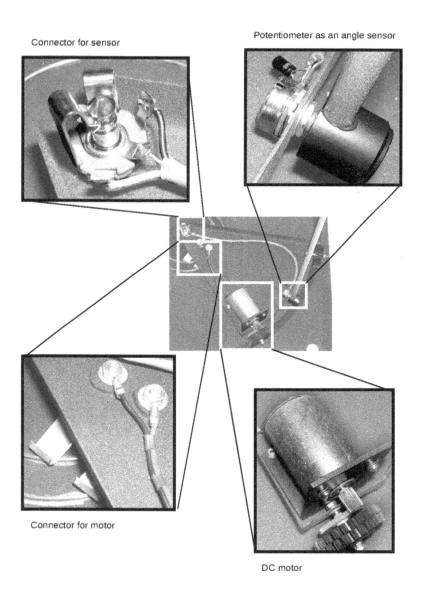

Figure 4.7. Connection between turning part and static part

Figure 4.8. Third version of inverted pendulum mechanical design

Because the third version has serial communication, the data can be read using computer.

The results are the system response from various Kp, Ki and Kd. Since the system output is angle, system response that is analyzed here is the angle error (difference between setpoint and measured value).

Through RS-232, the error of the pendulum is sent to computer for data logging. DataLogger II is used as software in computer to capture the data from microcontroller.

All graphs in this chapter use x-axis to represent time, and y-axis to represent degree. One block in x-axis is 500ms, and one block in y-axis is 7°.

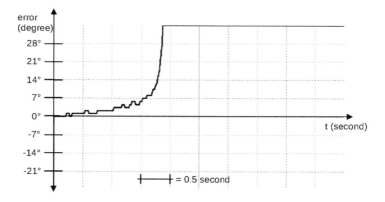

Figure 4.9. System response with P=16, I=0, D=0

With only Proportional, the error increase exponentially.

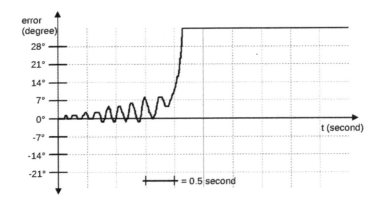

Figure 4.10. System response with P=20, I=0, D=0

With a higher Proportional gain, the system begins to oscillate. The error is still increase exponentially, but with oscillations.

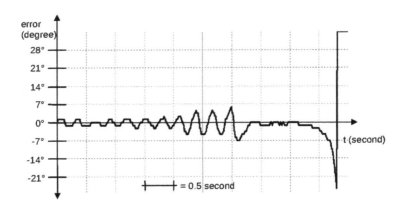

Figure 4.11. System response with P=16, I=1, D=0

With PI controller, the system is unstable. The oscillation is getting bigger.

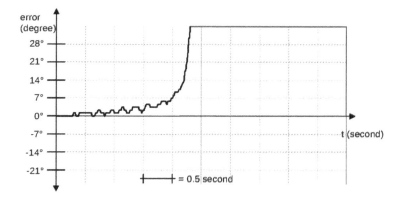

Figure 4.12. System response with P=16, I=0, D=3

With PD controller, the system is still unstable. The derivative term adds a little oscillation.

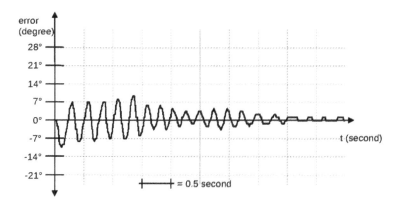

Figure 4.13. System response with P=16, I=1, D=3

With PID controller, the system is stable, but with many oscillations. To reduce the oscillations, Kd should be increased.

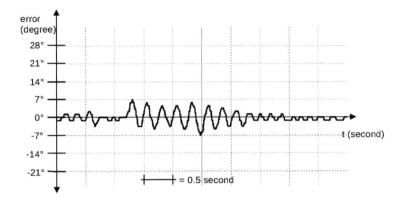

Figure 4.14. System response with P=16, I=1, D=4

This is the best result that can be achieved using PID controller. It is clear that oscillations still occur, but they are reduced by the increasing of Kd.

Chapter 5 – Conclusion and recommendation

Inverted pendulum can be controlled using digital PID controller. The system is stable, but with many oscillations. Oscillations occur because of big increment of PID constants. The use of integer cause the minimum increment is one. The increment cannot be in fraction.

Floating-point variable is highly suggested for the next project. With this method, smaller increment of Kp, Ki, and Kd can be obtained.

The graph for controller response can be added to analyze the controller behavior versus error.

REFERENCE

Text book

[1] Brey, B. B.(2002). *The Intel Microprocessors 8086/8088, 80186/80188, 80286, 80386, 80486, Pentium, Pentium Pro Processor, Pentium II, Pentium III, Pentium 4 Architecture, Programming, and Interfacing* (6th ed.). New Jersey: Prentice Hall.

[2] Ogata, K. (2001). *Modern Control Engineering* (3rd ed.). New Jersey: Prentice Hall.

[3] Rizzoni, G. (2002). *Principles and Applications of Electrical Engineering* (3rd ed.). New York: McGraw-Hill.

Manual, Datasheet, and Application Note

[4] Atmel. (2005). *ATmega8535(L) Datasheet* (Rev. G). Atmel Corporation.

[5] Atmel. (2002). *AVR108: Setup and Use of the LPM Instruction* (Rev. 1233B). Atmel Corporation.

[6] Atmel. (2002). *AVR201: Using the AVR® Hardware Multiplier* (Rev. 1631C). Atmel Corporation.

[7] Charais, J. & Lourens, R. (2004). *Software PID Control of an Inverted Pendulum Using the PIC16F684.* Microchip Technology Inc.

[8] Data Image. (2000). *GM24644SR-01 LCD Module Specification* (Rev. C). Data Image Corporation.

[9] Fairchild Semiconductor. (2001). *MC78XX/LM78XX/MC78XXA 3-Terminal 1A Positive Voltage Regulator Datasheet* (Rev. 1.0.1). Fairchild Semiconductor Corporation.

[10] STMicroelectronics. *L298 Dual Full Bridge Driver Datasheet.* STMicroelectronics.

Internet

[11] Craig, K. Awtar, S. (2004). *Inverted Pendulum Systems: Rotary and Arm-driven a Mechatronic System Design Case Study.* Retrieved: December 1, 2004, from http://web.mit.edu/~shorya/www/MS/craig_awtar_1.pdf.

[12] Dixor, R. (2005). *True Digital Control of an Inverted Pendulum System.* Retrieved: December 1, 2004, from http://www.es.lancs.ac.uk/cres/staff/rdixon/pendulum.html.

[13] ExperTune. (2005). *Comparison of PID Control Algoritms.* Retrieved: December 1, 2004, from http://www.expertune.com/articles.html.

[14] Lam, J. (2004). *Control of an Inverted Pendulum.* Retrieved: December 1, 2004, from http://www.ccec.ece.ucsb.edu/people/smith/student_projects/Johnny_Lam_report_238.pdf.

[15] Subbotin, Maxim. (2004). *Balancing an Inberted Pendulum on a Seesaw.* Retrieved: December 1, 2004, from http://www.ccec.ece.ucsb.edu/people/smith/student_projects/Subbotin_238_report.pdf.

[16] University of Michigan. (2004). *Example: Modeling an Inverted Pendulum.* Retrieved: November 30, 2004, from http://www.engin.umich.edu/group/ctm/examples/pend/invpen.html.

[17] University of Michigan. (2004). *Example: Solution to the Inverted Pendulum Problem Using PID Control.* Retrieved: November 30, 2004, from http://www.engin.umich.edu/group/ctm/examples/pend/invPID.html.

[18] University of Newcastle. (2004). *Inverted Pendulum Tutorial.* Retrieved: January 12, 2004, from http://csd.newcastle.edu.au/control/simulations/pend_sim.html.

[19] Wikipedia The Free Encyclopedia. (2005). *Atmel AVR.* Retrieved July 3 2005, from http://en.wikipedia.org/wiki/AVR.

[20] Wikipedia The Free Encyclopedia. (2005). *PID Controller.* Retrieved June
     23, 2005, from http://en.wikipedia.org/wiki/PID_controller.

GLOSSARY

Atmel AVR is a family of RISC microcontrollers from Atmel.

ADC is an analog-to-digital converter (abbreviated ADC, A/D, or A to D) is a device that converts continuous signals to discrete digital numbers.

Aliasing is an effect that causes different continuous signals to become indistinguishable (or aliases of one another) when sampled. When this happens, the original signal cannot be uniquely reconstructed from the sampled signal.

baud is a measure of the "signaling rate" which is the number of changes to the transmission media per second in a modulated signal.

EEPROM (Electrically-Erasable Programmable Read-Only Memory), is a non-volatile storage chip used in computers and other devices.

Feedback is a process whereby some proportion or in general, function, of the output signal of a system is passed (fed back) to the input.

Floating point is a digital representation for a number in a certain subset of the rational numbers, and is often used to approximate an arbitrary real number on a computer.

Integer consist of the positive natural numbers (1, 2, 3, ...), their negatives (−1, −2, −3, ...) and the number zero.

Oscillation is the periodic variation, typically in time, of some measure as seen, for example, in a swinging pendulum. The term vibration is sometimes used more narrowly to mean a mechanical oscillation but sometimes is used to be synonymous with oscillation.

PWM (Pulse-width modulation) of a signal or power source involves the modulation of its duty cycle to either convey information over a communications channel or control the amount of power sent to a load.

PID is a standard feedback loop component in industrial control applications.

RAM (random access memory) is a type of computer storage whose contents can be accessed in any (i.e., random) order. This is in contrast to sequential memory devices such as magnetic tapes, discs and drums, in which the mechanical movement of the storage medium forces the computer to access data in a fixed order.

ROM (Read-only memory) is used as a storage medium in computers. Because it cannot (easily) be written to, its main uses lie in the distribution of firmware (software that is very closely related to hardware, and not likely to need frequent upgrading).

RISC is a microprocessor CPU design philosophy that favors a smaller and simpler set of instructions that all take about the same amount of time to execute.

Sensor is a technological device or biological organ that detects, or senses, a signal or physical condition and chemical compounds

Serial communications is the process of sending data one bit at one time, sequentially, over a communications channel or computer bus. This is in contrast to parallel communications, where all the bits of each symbol are sent together

Setpoint is the target value that an automatic control system, for example PID controller, will aim to reach.

REVISION HISTORY

Add footnote in abstract, page 3.

Add educational title for lecturer in acknowledgements, page 5.

Add Edward B. Manurung M. Eng. in acknowledgements, page 5.

Add numbering to equation, page 13, 14, and 38.

Change figure 2.4 DC motor schematic diagram, page 19.

Change figure 2.5 PWM pulse, page 20.

Change figure 2.7 H-Bridge, page 22.

Add more points in reference, page 53 and 54.

Add revision history, page 57.

Add technical drawing, page 72, 73, and 74.

Add bill of material, page 75.

Remove empty pages.

APPENDIX A: Inverted pendulum program

```
.include "m8535def.inc" ;Includes the ATmega8535 definition file

.def templ = r16
.def temph = r17

.def tem1l = r18
.def tem1h = r19

;memory map
;setp(60,61)
;sensor(62,63)
;err(64,65)
;sumerr(66,67)
;errlast(68,69)
;kp(6a,6b)
;ki(6c,6d)
;kd(6e,6f)
;PID(70,71)
.cseg
.org 0x0000

;//////////////////////defining interupt vectors\\\\\\\\\\\\\\\\\\\\\
      rjmp reset
      reti; rjmp ext_int0
      reti; rjmp ext_int1
      rjmp tim2_comp
      reti; rjmp tim2_ovf
      reti; rjmp tim1_capt
      reti; rjmp tim1_compa
      reti; rjmp tim1_compb
      reti; rjmp tim1_ovf
      reti; rjmp tim0_ovf
      reti; rjmp spi_stc
      reti; rjmp usart_rxc
      reti; rjmp usart_udre
      reti; rjmp usart_txc
      reti; rjmp analog
      reti; rjmp ee_rdy
      reti; rjmp ana_comp
      reti; rjmp twsi
      reti; rjmp ext_int2
      reti; rjmp tim0_comp
      reti; rjmp spm_rdy

;----------------subroutines for interrupt request----------------
tim2_comp:
      ldi templ, (1<<refs0)|(1<<adlar)
      out admux, templ               ;ADC right adjusted, Vref=AVcc,
                                     ;ADC0 singgle ended
      ldi templ, (1<<se)|(1<<sm0)
      out mcucr, templ               ;sleep enable, ADC noise
                                     ;reduction
      sei                            ;nested interap
      sleep                          ;begin to convert ADC
      clr templ
      out mcucr, templ               ;sleep disable
```

```
        in templ, adch                  ;read the ADC result
        sts $0062, templ                ;move the ADC result to the
                                        ;memory
        ldi templ, 0x00
        sts $0063, templ

        lds templ, $0062                ;sensorL(62)
        lds temph, $0063                ;sensorH(63)
        lds tem1l, $0060                ;setpL(60)
        lds tem1h, $0061                ;setpH(61)

        sub templ, tem1l                ;sensorL(62) - setpL(60)
        sbc  temph, tem1h               ;sensorH(63) - setpH(61)
        ;max  and  min  errors  allowed  are  <0b00011011(0x1b)  or
        ;>0b11100110(0xe6)
        cpi templ, 0x1b
        brlo next
        cpi templ, 0xe6
        brsh next
        rjmp collapse

next:
        sts $0064, templ                ;save to errL(64)
        sts $0065, temph                ;save to errH(65)

;Proportional
        lds r22, $006a                  ;loading kp(6a,6b)
        lds r23, $006b
        lds r20, $0064                  ;loading err(64,65)
        lds r21, $0065
        rcall mul16x16_16               ;r17:r16 = r23:r22 * r21:r20
        sts $0070, r16                  ;save the result to PID(70,71)
        sts $0071, r17

;Integral
        lds r20, $0066                  ;loading sumerr(66,67)
        lds r21, $0067
        lds r22, $0064                  ;loading err(64,65)
        lds r23, $0065
        add r20, r22                    ;sumerr=sumerr+err
        adc r21, r23
        sts $0066, r20                  ;store sumerr(66,67) to sram
        sts $0067, r21
        lds r22, $006c                  ;loading ki(6c,6d)
        lds r23, $006d
        rcall mul16x16_16               ;r17:r16 = r23:r22 * r21:r20
        lds r18, $0070                  ;loading PID(70,71)
        lds r19, $0071
        add r18, r16                    ;PID=PID+integral
        adc r19, r17
        sts $0070, r18                  ;store PID to sram
        sts $0071, r19

;Derivative
        lds r20, $0064                  ;loading err(64,65)
        lds r21, $0065
        movw r17:r16, r21:r20
        lds r18, $0068                  ;loading errlast(68,69)
        lds r19, $0069
        sub r20, r18                    ;err=err-errlast
```

```
        sbc  r21, r19
        sts  $0068 ,r16              ;errlast is updated
        sts  $0069 ,r17
        lds  r22, $006e             ;loading kd(6e,6f)
        lds  r23, $006f
        rcall mul16x16_16           ;r17:r16 = r23:r22 * r21:r20
        lds  r18, $0070             ;loading PID(70,71)
        lds  r19, $0071
        add  r18, r16               ;PID=PID+derivative
        adc  r19, r17
        sts  $0070, r18             ;store PID to sram
        sts  $0071, r19


        cpi  r19, 0x80              ;PID limiter
        brsh minus                  ;because PWM will only accept 0-
                                    ;255
        brlo plus
minus:
        cpi  r18, 0x81
        brlo cond2
        rjmp motor
cond2:
        ldi  r18, 0x81
        rjmp motor
plus:
        cpi  r18, 0x80
        brsh cond1
        rjmp motor
cond1:
        ldi  r18, 0x80
        rjmp motor


motor:
        ldi  templ, 0x7f
        add  r18, templ             ;PID conditioner (unsign int to
                                    ;PWM)
        out  ocr0, r18             ;change the duty cycle of PWM
        clr  templ                 ;tell the main program to restart
        reti

;--------------end of subroutine for interrupt request--------------


;////////////////////////////////initialization\\\\\\\\\\\\\\\\\\\\\\\\\\
reset:                              ;<-------RESET
;stack initialization
        ldi  templ, high(ramend)
        out  sph, templ
        ldi  templ, low(ramend)
        out  spl, templ

;enabling global interupt
        sei

;ADC initialization
        ldi  templ, (1<<refs0)|(1<<adlar)
        out  admux, templ          ;ADC left adjusted,  Vref=AVcc,
                                    ;ADC0 singgle ended
        ldi  templ, (1<<aden)|(1<<adie)|(1<<adps2)|(1<<adps0)
```

```
        out adcsra, templ               ;ADC  enable,  prescaler=32,  ADC
                                        ;interupt enable

;identify set point
        ldi templ, (1<<se)|(1<<sm0)
        out mcucr, templ                ;sleep enable, ADC noise
                                        ;reduction

        again:
        sleep                           ;start ADC convertion
        in templ, adch                  ;read the ADC result
        rcall delay
        sleep                           ;start ADC convertion
        in temph, adch                  ;read the ADC result

        cp templ, temph                 ;compare the first  result  with
                                        ;the second one
        brne again                      ;if different repeat the identify
                                        ;proccess

        clr tem1l
        out mcucr, tem1l                ;sleep disable

;defining set point from sensor
        sts $0060, templ                ;setpL
        ldi templ, 0x00                 ;setpH=0x00
        sts $0061, templ                ;setpH

;Timer0 initialization (for PWM)
        ldi templ, (1<<toie0)
        out timsk, templ                ;Timer interrupt overflow enable
        ldi templ, (1<<wgm00)|(1<<com01)|(1<<com00)|(1<<cs01)|(1<<cs00)
        out tccr0, templ                ;PWM phase correct, set on
                                        ;counting up, 32 prescaler
        ldi templ, 128
        out ocr0, templ                 ;initial  value  for  PWM  (motor
                                        ;stop)

;Timer2 initialization (for sampling rate)
        ldi templ, (1<<ocie2)
        out timsk, templ                ;Timer interrupt on compare match
        ldi templ, 0x81
        out ocr2, templ                 ;compare match on 0x81 (=15Hz)
        ldi templ, (1<<wgm21)|(7<<cs20)
        out tccr2, templ                ;CTC, 1024 prescaler

;defining port d and oc0 as output
        ldi templ, 0xff
        out ddrd, templ
        sbi ddrb, 3
        out ddrc, templ

;initial value for PID variables
        clr templ
        ldi r28, 0x64                   ;point to address 0064
        clr r29                         ;point to address 0064
        ldi temph, 0x0e                 ;down counting for pointer y
        a:
        st   y+, templ                  ;err, sumerr, errlast = 0
        dec temph                       ;kp, ki, kd = 0
```

```
      brne a                          ;PID = 0

;RS-232 initialization
      ldi templ, 12
      out ubrrl, templ                ;baud rate = 19200, error = 0.2%
      ldi templ, 0
      out ubrrh, templ                ;baud rate = 19200, error = 0.2%
      ldi templ, (1<<ursel)|(2<<upm0)|(1<<usbs)|(3<<ucsz0)
      out ucsrc, templ                ;async., even parity, 2 stop bit,
                                      ;char. size = 8
      ldi templ, (1<<txen)
      out ucsrb, templ                ;transmitter enable

;LCD initializtion
      ;LCD reset
      ldi templ, 0b01010100
      out portd, templ
      rcall delay

      ;display mode
      ldi templ, 0b10010100           ;graph on, text off, cursor off,
                                      ;blink off
      rcall command0

      ;mode set
      ldi templ, 0x80                 ;AND=0x83, OR=0x80
      rcall command0

      ;graphic home address
      ;ldi templ, 0x00
      ;ldi temph, 0x00
      ;ldi tem11, 0x42
      ;rcall command2

      ;graphic area
      ;ldi templ, 0x1e
      ;ldi temph, 0x00
      ;ldi tem11, 0x43
      ;rcall command2

      ;text home address
      ldi templ, 0x00                 ;defining text home address
      ldi temph, 0x00
      ldi tem11, 0x44
      rcall command2

      ;text area
      ldi templ, 0x1e                 ;defining text area
      ldi temph, 0x00
      ldi tem11, 0x45
      rcall command2

      ;address pointer
      ldi templ, 0x00                 ;defining address pointer
      ldi temph, 0x00
      ldi tem11, 0x24
      rcall command2

      ldi templ, 0xb0
      rcall command0                  ;autowrite(e)
```

```
        ldi zh, high (prop<<1)          ;loading LCD frame
        ldi zl, low (prop<<1)
        jik:
        lpm templ, z+
        ldi temph, 0x20
        sub templ, temph
        cpi templ, 0x58
        rcall awrite
        brne jik

        ldi templ, 0xb2
        rcall command0                  ;autoreset

;go to main program
        rjmp start

;\\\\\\\\\\\\\\\\\\\\\end of initialization////////////////////////



;------------------------------------------------------
;********************MAIN PROGRAM********************
;------------------------------------------------------

start:
;read from ADC1 (proportional)
        ldi templ, (1<<refs0)|(1<<adlar)|(1<<mux0)
        out admux, templ                ;Vref=AVcc, ADC left adjusted,
                                        ;ADC1 singgle ended
        ldi templ, (1<<se)|(1<<sm0)
        out mcucr, templ                ;sleep enable, ADC noise
                                        ;reduction
        sleep
        clr templ
        out mcucr, templ                ;sleep disable
        in templ, adch
        lsr templ
        lsr templ
        sts $006a, templ

;read from ADC2 (integral)
        ldi templ, (1<<refs0)|(1<<adlar)|(1<<mux1)
        out admux, templ                ;Vref=AVcc, ADC left adjusted,
                                        ;ADC2 singgle ended
        ldi templ, (1<<se)|(1<<sm0)
        out mcucr, templ                ;sleep enable, ADC noise
                                        ;reduction
        sleep
        clr templ
        out mcucr, templ                ;sleep disable
        in templ, adch
        lsr templ
        lsr templ
        lsr templ
        lsr templ
        lsr templ
        sts $006c, templ
```

```
;read from ADC3 (derivative)
      ldi templ, (1<<refs0)|(1<<adlar)|(1<<mux1)|(1<<mux0)
      out admux, templ                  ;Vref=AVcc, ADC left adjusted,
                                        ;ADC3 singgle ended
      ldi templ, (1<<se)|(1<<sm0)
      out mcucr, templ                  ;sleep enable, ADC noise
                                        ;reduction
      sleep
      clr templ
      out mcucr, templ                  ;sleep disable
      in templ, adch
      lsr templ
      lsr templ
      lsr templ
      lsr templ
      sts $006e, templ

;read errorL and send through rs-232
      la1:
      sbis ucsra, udre
      rjmp la1                          ;check the usart availability
      lds templ, $0064                  ;loading error
      ldi temph, 128
      add templ, temph
      out udr, templ                    ;send error

;displaying PID, err, controller
      lds templ, $006a                  ;loading kp
      rcall hex                         ;converting hex -> ascii
      ;address pointer
      ldi templ, 0x4b
      ldi temph, 0x00
      ldi r23, 0x5f                     ;no sign
      rcall value

      lds templ, $006c                  ;loading ki
      rcall hex                         ;converting hex -> ascii
      ;address pointer
      ldi templ, 0x69
      ldi temph, 0x00
      ldi r23, 0x5f                     ;no sign
      rcall value

      lds templ, $006e                  ;loading kd
      rcall hex
      ;address pointer
      ldi templ, 0x87
      ldi temph, 0x00
      ldi r23, 0x5f                     ;no sign
      rcall value

      lds templ, $0064                  ;loading error
      cpi templ, 0x80                   ;and show it to LCD
      brsh minu
      rcall hex
      ;address pointer
      ldi templ, 0xa5
      ldi temph, 0x00
      ldi r23, 0x0b
      rcall value
```

```
      rjmp sk
      minu:
      ldi temph, 0xff
      muls templ, temph
      mov templ, r0
      rcall hex
      ;address pointer
      ldi templ, 0xa5
      ldi temph, 0x00
      ldi r23, 0x0d
      rcall value
      sk:

      lds templ, $0070              ;loading PID
      cpi templ, 0x80               ;and show it to LCD
      brsh minu1
      rcall hex
      ;address pointer
      ldi templ, 0xc3
      ldi temph, 0x00
      ldi r23, 0x0b
      rcall value
      rjmp sk1
      minu1:
      ldi temph, 0xff
      muls templ, temph
      mov templ, r0
      rcall hex
      ;address pointer
      ldi templ, 0xc3
      ldi temph, 0x00
      ldi r23, 0x0d
      rcall value
      sk1:

      ldi templ, 0x03
finish:
      cpi templ, 0x03
      breq finish

      rjmp start
;------------------------------------------------------
;***************END OF MAIN PROGRAM****************
;------------------------------------------------------


;///////////////////////////////Subroutines\\\\\\\\\\\\\\\\\\\\\\\\\\\\\\\

mul16x16_16:                        ;r17:r16 = r23:r22 * r21:r20
      mul    r22, r20               ; al * bl
      movw   r17:r16, r1:r0
      mul    r23, r20               ; ah * bl
      add    r17, r0
      mul    r21, r22               ; bh * al
      add    r17, r0
      ret

delay:
      ldi tem1l, 0x9
```

```
        del1:
        ldi tem1h, 0xff
        del:
        dec tem1h
        brne del
        dec tem1l
        brne del1
        ret

;-----=====LCD subroutine=====-----
command0:
        rcall stat
        out portc, templ
        ldi templ, 0x24
        out portd, templ                ;write, ce, command (0x24)
        ret

command2:
        rcall stat
        out portc, templ
        ldi templ, 0x20
        out portd, templ                ;read(d), write(e), ce(e), data
                                        ;(0x20)
        rcall stat
        out portc, temph
        ldi templ, 0x20
        out portd, templ                ;read(d), write(e), ce(e), data
                                        ;(0x20)
        rcall stat
        out portc, tem1l
        ldi templ, 0x24
        out portd, templ                ;write, ce, command (0x24)
        ret

awrite:
        rcall stat
        out portc, templ
        ldi templ, 0x20
        out portd, templ                ;read(d), write(e), ce(e), data
                                        ;(0x20)
        ret

write:
        rcall stat
        out portc, templ
        ldi templ, 0x20
        out portd, templ                ;read(d), write(e), ce(e), data
                                        ;(0x20)
        rcall stat
        ldi templ, 0xc0
        out portc, templ                ;write and adp increment
        ldi templ, 0x24
        out portd, templ                ;write, ce, command (0x24)
        ret

stat:
        push templ
        sbi portd, 3
        ldi templ, 0x00
        out portc, templ
```

```
        out ddrc, templ                 ;portc => input
        ldi templ, 0x14
        out portd, templ                ;read(e), write(d), ce(e),
                                        ;command
        t:
        sbis pinc, 0                    ;waiting for LCD ready
        rjmp t
        sbis pinc, 1                    ;waiting for LCD ready
        rjmp t
        sbi portd, 3
        ldi templ, 0xff
        out ddrc, templ                 ;portc => output
        pop templ
        ret
;-----=====end of LCD subroutine=====-----

value:                                  ;four output from r23, r22, r21,
                                        ;r20
        ldi tem1l, 0x24
        rcall command2                  ;set the position
        ldi templ, 0xb0
        rcall command0                  ;autowrite(e)
        mov templ, r23
        rcall awrite
        mov templ, r22
        rcall awrite
        mov templ, r21
        rcall awrite
        mov templ, r20
        rcall awrite
        ldi templ, 0xb2
        rcall command0                  ;autoreset
        ret

;hex to ASCII converter input=templ, out=r22 r21 r20
hex:
        cpi templ, 0x64
        brsh a1
        ldi r22, 0x5f
        rjmp second
        a1:
        cpi templ, 0xc8
        brsh a2
        ldi r22, 0x11
        ldi temph, 0x64
        sub templ, temph
        rjmp second
        a2:
        ldi r22, 0x12
        ldi temph, 0xc8
        sub templ, temph
        rjmp second

        second:
        cpi templ, 0x0a
        clr r21
        brsh a3
        ldi r21, 0x5f
        rjmp third
        a3:
```

```
        inc r21
        ldi temph, 0x0a
        mul r21, temph
        cp templ, r0
        brsh a3
        dec r21
        mul r21, temph
        sub templ, r0
        ldi tem1l, 0x10
        add r21, tem1l

        third:
        ldi tem1l, 0x10
        add templ, tem1l
        mov r20, templ
        ret

collapse:
        cli
        cbi ddrb, 3

        la2:
        sbis ucsra, udre
        rjmp la2                        ;check the usart availability
        ldi templ, 0xff
        out udr, templ                  ;send error = 255

        coll:
        nop
        nop
        nop
        nop
        rjmp coll
;/////////////////////////end of subroutines\\\\\\\\\\\\\\\\\\\\\\\\\\
;databyte
prop:
.db "   SGU Lab. INVERTED PENDULUM   "
.db "-----------------------------"
.db "Proportional =                 "
.db "Integral     =                 "
.db "Derivative   =                 "
.db "Error        =                 "
.db "Controller   =                 "
.db "                             x"
```

APPENDIX B: Relation between angle positions, length of pendulum, and angle acceleration [7]

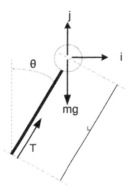

Figure B1. Inverted pendulum free body diagram

The length of the pendulum is from bottom to center of gravity of the pendulum (L).

The position of the pendulum can be represent with this equation

$position = iL \sin \theta + jL \cos \theta$

The first derivation of the position is velocity, and the second derivation is acceleration.

$velocity = iL \theta' \cos \theta - jL \theta' \sin \theta$

$acceleration = (iL \theta'' \cos \theta - iL \theta'^2 \sin \theta) - (jL \theta'' \sin \theta + jL \theta'^2 \cos \theta)$
$acceleration = L(i \theta'' \cos \theta - j \theta'' \sin \theta - i \theta'^2 \sin \theta - j \theta'^2 \cos \theta)$

There are two forces in the system, the first is occurred because the mass of the pendulum, and the second is rod tension.

$force = mL(i \theta'' \cos \theta - j \theta'' \sin \theta - i \theta'^2 \sin \theta - j \theta'^2 \cos \theta)$
$force = iT \sin \theta + jT \cos \theta - jmg$

The two equations can be combined together.

$$iT \sin\theta + jT \cos\theta - jmg = mL(i\theta'' \cos\theta - j\theta'' \sin\theta - i\theta'^2 \sin\theta - j\theta'^2 \cos\theta)$$

Separate i vector and j vector.

$$T \sin\theta = mL\theta'' \cos\theta - mL\theta'^2 \sin\theta$$

$$T \cos\theta - mg = -mL\theta'' \sin\theta - mL\theta'^2 \cos\theta$$

Multiply i vector with cos θ and j vector with sin θ.

$$T \sin\theta \cos\theta = mL\theta'' \cos^2\theta - mL\theta'^2 \sin\theta \cos\theta$$

$$T \sin\theta \cos\theta - mg \sin\theta = -mL\theta'' \sin^2\theta - mL\theta'^2 \sin\theta \cos\theta$$

Equations above can be combined.

$$mL\theta'' \cos^2\theta - mL\theta'^2 \sin\theta \cos = mg \sin\theta - mL\theta'' \sin^2\theta - mL\theta'^2 \sin\theta \cos$$

Divide by mL.

$$\theta'' \cos^2\theta - \theta'^2 \sin\theta \cos = \frac{g \sin\theta}{L} - \theta'' \sin^2\theta - \theta'^2 \sin\theta \cos$$

$$\theta'' (\cos^2\theta + \sin^2\theta) = \frac{g \sin\theta}{L}$$

$$\theta'' = \frac{g \sin\theta}{L}$$

APPENDIX C: Electrical circuit of DC motor driver

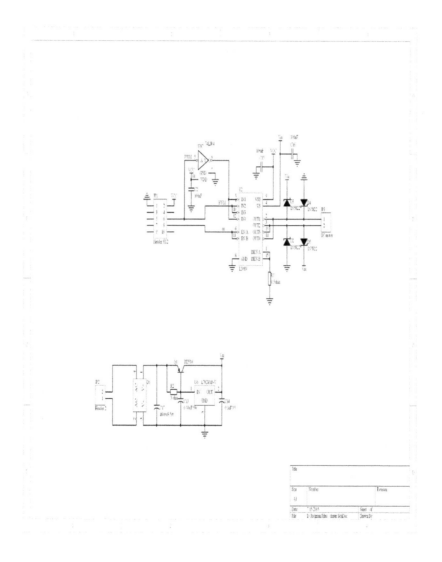

APPENDIX D: Technical drawing base

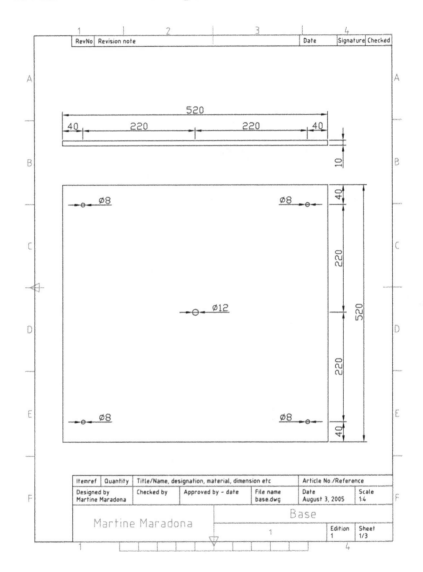

APPENDIX E: Technical drawing cart

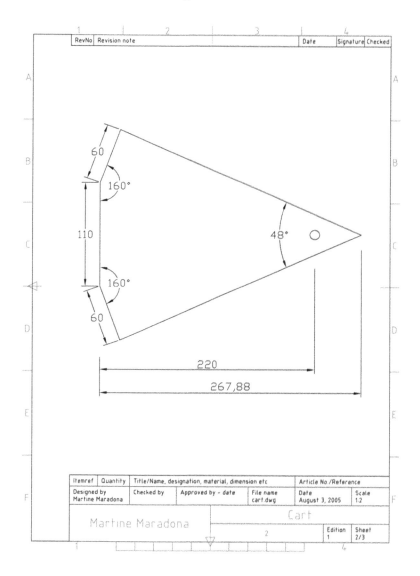

APPENDIX F: Technical drawing motor holder

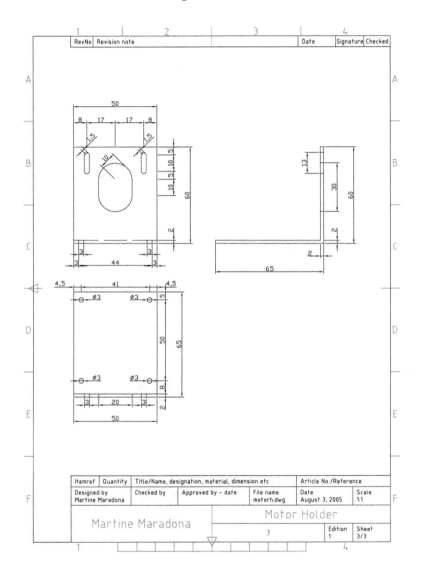

APPENDIX G: Bill of materials (BOM)

Qty	Material	Total price	
1	DT-AVR development board	Rp.	210.000
1	Graphic LCD GM24644	Rp.	150.000
1	L298N	Rp.	23.000
1	Motor driver PCB	Rp.	175.000
1	8mm stereo jack (f)	Rp.	25.500
1	8mm stereo jack (m)	Rp.	7.000
5	10k potentiometer	Rp.	15.000
4	1N5822	Rp.	40.000
1	7818	Rp.	1.500
1	acrylic 2mm	Rp.	10.000
3m	belden cable 8761	Rp.	18.000
1	TIP 42C	Rp.	5.000
1	74LS04	Rp.	2.000
1m	IDC cable 34	Rp.	17.000
3	100nF	Rp.	1.500
1	C 0.33uF/50v	Rp.	500
1	C 0.1uF/35v	Rp.	500
1	bridge diode	Rp.	3.000
1	C 4700uF/50v	Rp.	2.000
1	R 3ohm	Rp.	50
1	R 0.5ohm 5 watt	Rp.	1.000
1	3A transformer	Rp.	30.000

Total price		Rp.	737.550

CURRICULUM VITAE

Personal Information

Name	: Martine Maradona
Citizen	: Indonesia
Place of Birth	: Bandung
Birth Date	: November 26, 1982
Address	: Thamrin 20, Semarang
Telephone Number	: +62 24 747 3880
Cellular	: +62 8159125064
Email	: mart_maradona@yahoo.com

Work Experiences

August 6 – November 22, 2002

Internship at NVTDC (National Vocational Training Development Centre),
Bandung - West Java with training material:

    a. Electrical:

        Harnessing

        Soldering

        Basic Electrical

        Basic Electronics

        Power Supply

        Lay Out 3 Phases

    b. Mechanics:

        Bench Work

        Sheet Metal

        Measurement

        Basic Turning & Milling

        Robot Components Production with manual machine

        Assembling

Passing grade: good

February 2 – August 26, 2004

Internship at Herrenknecht, Schwanau – Germany

- Wrote a manual book for a vertical shaft drilling machine

- Involved in drilling project in Gunung Kidul – Jogjakarta

Education

Formal education

Year	School/College/University	Degree	Subject
1987-1989	Bernardus	Kindergarten	General
1989-1995	Bernardus	Elementary	General
1995-1998	Domenico Savio	Junior High	General
1998-2001	Kolese Loyola	Senior High	Science
2001-2005	Swiss German University	Bachelor	Mechatronics

Course

Certificate Date	Institution Organiser	Course Theme
August 2, 2000	LPK Budiman	Elementary Computer Technician
March 28, 2002	Swiss German University	Build Computer from Scratch
January 20, 2003	ELKA COM	Computer Technician II

Seminar

Date	Institution Organizer	Seminar Title
April 20, 2002	Swiss German University	Go wireless!
March 16, 2002	Swiss German University	Voice over Internet Protocol

Language Skills

Bahasa Indonesia – mother tongue

English – intermediate

Martine Maradona

German Language – beginner

Computer Skills

MS Office – Intermediate

MS Windows – Advance

Computer Hardware – Advance

Linux – Beginner